ABC MATH Riddles

by
Jannelle Martin

illustrations by
Freddie Levin

An ABC Riddles book from

Peel Productions

To Al, who is truly wonderful.

— *J. M.*

To my Dad, who patiently taught me
multiplication tables at home,
after I spent third grade math time
drawing.

— *F. L.*

Text copyright©2003 Jannelle Martin
Illustrations copyright©2003 Freddie Levin0

Published by Peel Productions, Inc.
PO Box 546, Columbus NC 28722
http://peelbooks.com

Printed in China

Library of Congress Cataloging-in-Publication Data
Martin, Jannelle.
  ABC math riddles / by Jannelle Martin ; illustrated by Freddie Levin.
      p. cm.
Summary: A collection of twenty-six riddles, one for each letter of
the alphabet, that describe mathematical operations, shapes, and
other concepts and ask the reader "What am I?"
  ISBN 0-939217-57-0 (alk. paper)
  1. Mathematics—Terminology—Juvenile literature. 2.
Riddles—Juvenile literature. [1. Mathematics. 2. Riddles.] I. Levin,
Freddie, ill. II. Title.
  QA41.3 .M37 2003
  510'.1'4—dc21
                              2003001750

a_ _

A three-letter word, I start with an A.
The plus sign with me shows you the way.
To find a total, I'm what you do
when you take one plus one and get two.
You use me everyday.
What's my name? Can you say?

b_ _ _ _ _w

B is my beginning and W is my end.
Useful in subtracting,
I'm the opposite of lend.
I help find the answer
to twenty minus three.
Can you guess my name now?
What word can I be?

c _ _ _ t

I start with a C and end with a T.
If you want to use me,
say "One, two, three..."
Use me to figure money,
birthday candles too.
Can you guess what I am?
If you can, please do.

d_____e

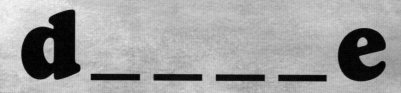

D begins my name, it ends with an E.
To split a whole into parts,
you can use me
when you want to share
a pizza at the fair.
I'm the opposite of multiply.
What's my name? Who am I?

e_ _ _

A certain type of number, I start with an E.
The opposite of odd, I am never number three.
You use my type of number
when you count by twos.
What kind of number am I?
Can you guess from the clues?

f_ _ _

My name starts with F,
three more letters belong.
Use me to measure something wide or long.
It takes twelve inches to make one of me,
so with thirty-six inches my total is three.
Sometimes you put my word in a shoe.
Do you know who I am? Say, if you do.

g_ _ _ _ _ _

My name has seven letters,
it starts with a G.
I am larger than the other
amount you can see.
Just think of the bigger
when two sizes you compare.
If you choose me,
you will get the bigger share.
I rhyme with later.
I'm the opposite of lesser,
Can you guess my name?
If so, what a guesser.

h _ _ _

My name starts with H,
there are three letters more.
One of two equal parts, also two out of four.
I'm thirty minutes of an hour
and fifty cents of a dollar.
Do you know my fraction name?
Say it loud, but do not holler!

i_ _ _

I is the first letter
of my four letter word.
Used to measure length,
my name is often heard.
An insect by my name
is a green, squiggly worm.
Can you guess my name?
Please do, but don't squirm?

j_gg_ _

Beginning with a J, I also have two G's.
I'm sometimes used to move
numbers where you please.
I'm also done with objects
under the circus tent.
I'm sure you know my name.
Do you know what word is meant?

k _ _ _

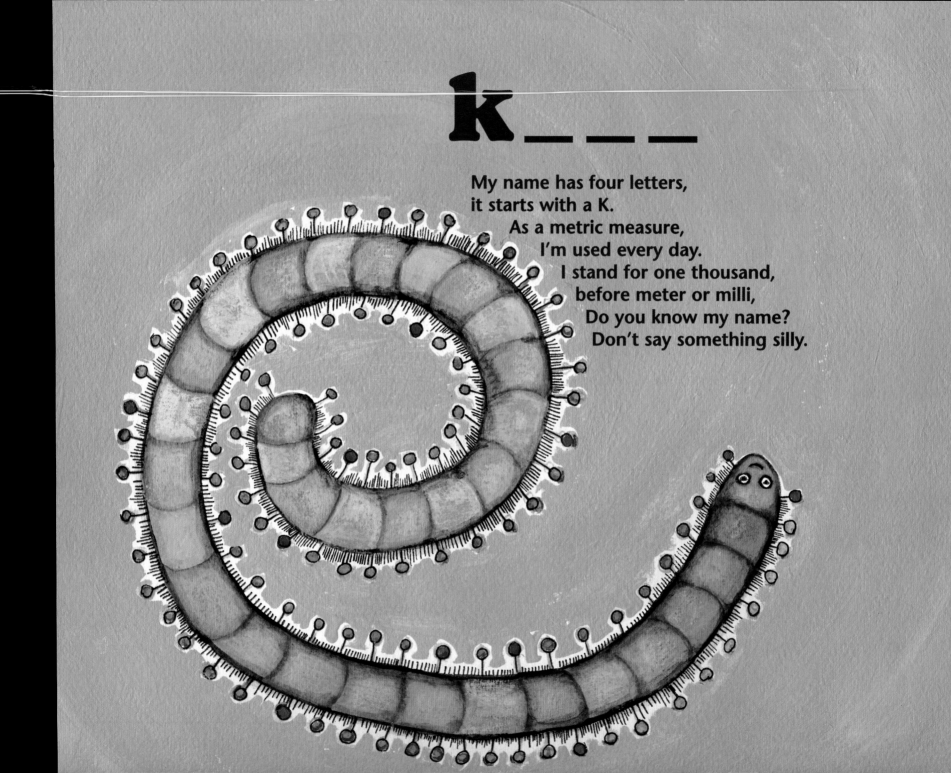

My name has four letters,
it starts with a K.
As a metric measure,
I'm used every day.
I stand for one thousand,
before meter or milli,
Do you know my name?
Don't say something silly.

l _ _ e

My name begins with L,
there's an E at the end.
I'm a set of points,
and I will never bend.
Some think I curve.
Some think I swerve.
But I am always straight.
What am I? Please state!

m_____y

M is my first letter and Y is my last.
Use me to get totals, simple and fast.
I'm related to addition, like two + two + two.
If you use my times sign (X), three times two will do.
I'll help you find the answer to five times sixty-three.
What math operation am I? What word must I be?

n_____l

Starting with an N
and ending with an L,
I'm the symbol for amounts you know well.
I can look like a six or seventy-three,
or any quantity you want me to be.
Some people think "number"
and my word are the same.
Can you name me now?
You are good at this game.

O_ _

A three letter word, I start with an O.
I'm a special type of number, as this riddle will show.
Some examples of me are five and eleven,
not two, four, or six; but yes to seven.
An even number I am not.
Did you figure me out?
What have you got?

P_ _ _ _

A measure of weight, I begin with a P.
A scale shows my total, one, two, three.
Two thousand of me makes one ton.
Sixteen ounces will equal only one.
How many of me can an elephant be?
What am I? Can you name me?

q _ _ _ t

I begin with a Q and end with a T.
Use my unit of measure in a recipe,
when you're making cakes
or shaking lots of shakes.
Not a gallon, not a pint,
I'm something in between.
Can you guess my name?
If so, you are keen.

r _ _ t _ _ _ _ _ _

R begins my name, there's also a T.
I'm a four-sided shape, found in geometry.
My opposite sides are the same exact length.
Four right angle corners give me my strength.
Neither a square nor a circle am I.
Can you name my shape?
Give it a try.

s _ _ _ _ _ _ t

I begin with an S and end with a T.
I'm the same as "take-away" as you will soon see.
If you have six bananas and then you eat two,
you still have four left. What math did you do?
After using me, your total will be less.
I'm the opposite of add. Can you guess?

t_____e

My name starts with a T and ends with an E.
A three-sided shape, my angles total three.
Find my shape in a scarf made for your head
or in half a cheese sandwich,
made on toasted bread.
My shape is found in the top of an A.
Do you know my name? If so, please say.

_u___ __

There's a U in my name,
four more letters belong.
I'm used to measure, something short or long.
As a stick, I work great
to help make lines straight.
My marks measure inches,
         centimeters, or feet.
      Can you guess my name?
      Guessing right is a treat.

v_____l

I start with a V, there's an L at the end.
I'm straight up and down and I never bend.
Like a skyscraper high,
I point to the sky.
Power poles point up like me.
What, oh what, can I be?

w_ _ _ _t

I start with a W and end with a T.
I tell you how heavy something might be.
Measure me in units of ounces or pounds,
grams or milligrams, there are no bounds.
To find my amount, you can use a scale.
What is my name? Guess now, you can't fail.

h _ x _ _ _ _ _

H starts my name, X fills the third space.
My straight sides make my unique base.
A triangle I'm not,
six angles I've got.
A polygon fine, I'm a special design.
Can you give it a try? What shape am I?

y_ _ _

A four letter word, I begin with a Y.
Use me to find the width or length of something high.
The same as thirty-six inches, I'm also three feet.
I can figure how far you walk to your street.
I'm also the name of a measuring stick.
What am I called? What name do you pick?

Z_ _ _

Four letters long, I start with a Z.
I'm a special number, as you will see.
If you have one balloon, that is not so many;
but it's more than I am, because I am not any.
When I stand alone, I stand for none.
Guess my name and then you are done.

a_____s

We start with an A and end with an S.
We say what's correct. What did you guess?

add	juggle	subtract
borrow	kilo	triangle
count	line	ruler
divide	multiply	vertical
even	numeral	weight
foot	odd	hexagon
greater	pound	yard
half	quart	zero
inch	rectangle	

Ideas for Parents and Teachers

Creating math riddles that rhyme is a wonderful way to explore the connection between the world of math and the worlds of reading, writing, the arts, and the environment. Here are some ideas for enhancing your enjoyment of this book.

- Instruct children to wait until all clues have been given before guessing the riddle. Have the child who guesses the answer first say the correct word, spell it out, then choose a new math riddle to read.

- Create math riddles! Let children choose something they are curious about. Begin with letter and word clues. Look up definitions in the dictionary to make sure you've got the just-right words. Pay attention to rhythm as well as rhymes. End each riddle with a question, inviting others to answer your riddle.

  Start with a simple riddle such as this one for square:

  I am a shape that begins with an S.
  I have four equal sides. What is your guess?

- Share riddles! You can give them to someone else to read or you can perform them in front of others. Another way to share your riddle is to set it to music!

- As extended activities, encourage children to draw or sculpt the subjects of their riddles. For ideas, look for math concepts and shapes in the world around you—at school, at home, in the city, in the country, in the arts, and in nature.

Have fun!

m _ _ _

A subject you study,
I begin with an M.
I'm a favorite in school,
perhaps the best of them.
My lessons teach time
and how to measure,
numbers, shapes, fractions—
whatever your pleasure.
You can use what you learn,
your whole life through.
Can you guess my name?
It's easy with this clue.

If you've enjoyed this book, look for
others on our web site

http://peelbooks.com

or at your favorite bookseller